Margaret Wise Brown

THE Little Fireman

Pictures by Esphyr Slobodkina

Young Scott Books

Once upon a time there was

a great big tall fireman.

And once upon a
time there was a
little fireman.

They lived in two fire houses
right next door to each other.

And one fireman had a big
black and white dalmatian
puppy dog who ran behind his
fire engine to the fires.

And the other fireman had a very little black and white dalmatian puppy dog who ran to all the fires right behind his little fire engine.

One night the two firemen were sleeping in their fire houses and the dalmatian puppy dogs were sleeping under their fire engines.

When clang!
went the loud
ringing noise
of the fire
gong in the
big fire house,

and cling! went
the little ringing
noise of the fire
gong in the little
fireman's house.

Bow-wow-wow barked the big dalmatian dog!

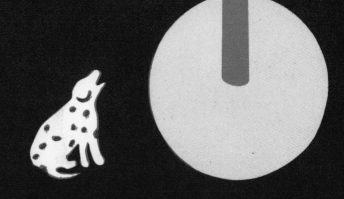

Yip! yip! yip! barked the little dalmatian dog!

"Fire! fire! fire!"

called the people in the streets.

Then out from the big fire house came the big fireman in his big fire engine with his big dalmatian dog running behind him.

And out from the little fire house came the little fireman with his little puppy dog running along behind him.

Clang! clang! clang!

Cling! cling! cling!

And down
the street
a couple
of blocks,
and down
a street to
the right,
there was
a great
big house
on fire!

When the big fireman got there, he said:
"Ho! ho! what a fine big roaring fire!"

*But when the little fireman got to the fire, he said:
"Oh dear! oh dear! that fire is too big for me!"*

And then down the street two blocks, and on a block to the left, he saw a very little house on fire!

So cling! cling! cling! off he went
down the street to the little fire.

And there in
the windows of
the little house
were fifteen
very little fat
ladies calling
"Help! Help!"

And they all
jumped out of
the windows
to the little
fireman who
caught them
in a little net.

At the big fire there were fifteen big fat ladies in the windows

**and they all jumped out and the big
fireman caught them in his big net.**

When the big
fire was all
splashed out
with water,

and when the little fire was

all splashed out with water,

The two firemen jumped in their fire engines and went
home with the
dalmatian
puppy dogs
running along
behind them.

The big fireman ate a great big mutton chop and a great big dish of pink ice cream; then he jumped into bed and went right to sleep.

And the little fireman ate a very little mutton chop and a very little dish of pink ice cream; then he jumped into bed and went right to sleep.

And the great big fireman

dreamed a very little dream.

And
the little
fireman dreamed
a great big dream.

juv. 81-1352

Brown, Margaret Wise

The Little Fireman.

juv. 81-1352

Brown, Margaret Wise

AUTHOR

The Little Fireman.

TITLE

DATE DUE	BORROWER'S NAME
FEB 18	B. Russell
FEB 24	J. Boomhower
DEC 7	Gregg Zachrich
JUL 10 '84	Shanna Dai...